For C
... as inspired by
Anthea's songs

Victoria
Christmas 2013

Beautiful Soups
© Kate Dyson, 2012

All rights reserved.

No part of this publication may be reproduced, stored in a retrieval system by any means, electronic, mechanical, photocopying, recording or otherwise, without the prior written permission of the publishers and copyright holders.

ISBN 978-178035-236-7
First published 2012 by
FASTPRINT PUBLISHING
Peterborough, England

Hotties and Mothers' Hugs...

BEAUTIFUL SOUPS

Kate Dyson

Illustrated by Jemima Mills
Cover photography by John Dyson

Memories of happy meals
at our family table

For

John
Jemima
Jenny
Jack
Kinna

"The family that eats together stays together."

Mohinder Singh

FOREWORD

Three scruffy old notebooks live in my kitchen. Over many years, I have scribbled down recipes in them. Cooking is my relaxation. It is the perfect way to calm the mind after a busy day in my shop. Slicing and dicing, stirring and baking helps me to change tune between work and home, whether there are one or two at home, or a gaggle. Doing Mother and Grandmother stuff with grandchildren around also makes for happy cooking.

With all four children leading grown-up lives, with sons-in-law and grandchildren, the family and friends have asked me to put these skeleton recipe notes into a form that they can read. This is the first in a series of little books which will form a compendium of all kinds of recipes – from soups to puddings.

For many years, before starting The Dining Room Shop in 1985, I worked as an antiques journalist. I ran a small newspaper at one stage where the best fun was writing a regular feature on food and antiques. This involved researching old recipes, recreating them and serving them up in the original dishes that might have been on the table at the time when the books were published. This fascination with yesterday's food and yesterday's dishes led to the start of my shop, and endless chats with customers about foody matters and the best ways of dishing up meals that both look and taste delicious.

In this first book, there is a mixture of the antique and the personal. Use it for ideas. The recipes do not have to be followed slavishly. If there are no onions in the fridge, for example, use leeks instead. So… Substitute… Experiment… Relax… Above all…. enjoy.

Kate
London, 2012

CONTENTS

3	Introduction	42	Green pepper and lettuce soup
7	Making stocks	44	Mixed vegetable soup
13	All sorts of soup recipes	46	Fridge art soup
14	Soothing fish soup	48	Flavourings and fridge art soups
16	Barley and vegetable broth	49	Garnishes
18	Curried avocado soup	50	Tomato soup
20	Pumpkin soup	52	Tomato and fennel soup
22	Noodle soup	54	Lentil and celery soup
24	Bren's fish soup	56	Curried apple soup
26	Coconut chicken noodle soup	58	Hedgehog soup
28	Weekend soup with lemon grass	60	Minestrone
30	Courgette and couscous soup	64	French onion soup
32	Wedding plan soup	66	Borscht
34	Chicken broth with parsley and parmesan	68	Gazpacho
36	Parsnip soup	70	Bloody Mary soup
38	Celery soup	72	Professica's okra soup
40	Courgette and lemon soup	74	Historical notes
		76	Soup is served
		78	The soup tureen

INTRODUCTION

For comfort eating, soup outshines everything. A chilly day, a hot mug of homemade soup, a crust of fresh warm brown bread naughtily crowned with a sun-hat of butter is my idea of eating heaven. It's the food equivalent of a hotty and a mother's hug.

At home, except in boiling weather, there is generally a pan of soup on the go. It's there when my husband has his lunch break. Emerging from his typewriter, he props up the kitchen bench and sips his mug of soup – preferably something a bit vegetably with a snatch of hot seasoning and a slice of toast. He does the crossword, polishes off the soup and watches garden birds nabbing sunflower seeds from the feeder hanging outside the window. Then it's back to his office, brain well-fuelled for an afternoon's writing.

Soup is also there for itinerant children and their friends at all hours of the day and night. After school they would curl up on the kitchen sofa with a mug of soup to watch the television. Or they would steal back on tiptoes, late from a party, probably having had too much to drink and forgotten to eat supper, so the fridge was raided. Soup has always been considered the perfect midnight feast and night cap. Kinna, youngest daughter, says soup is better than eggs and bacon or cereal for breakfast, especially if it is carrot and even more especially if she has overslept on Sunday morning.

Soup helps you to produce all sorts of nourishing meals in a bowl or mug without too much clashing of batterie de cuisine. A good dollop of stock, a handful of noodles, broken in to shorter pieces, a dash of Soy, plus freshly chopped herbs – this is one of the quickest lunchtime dishes you can make – a trying-to-be authentic Chinese recipe that takes no more than 10 to 15 minutes. Or add to the stock a generous scattering of chopped parsley and of grated carrots, with a tablespoon of softened garlic and onion – this makes a fortifying broth – even more so if you add a handful of barley and cook for a bit longer. The resulting taste is a bit like being kissed by a favourite maiden aunt with big bosoms – wholesome and deeply loving with no strings attached.

For a swift minestrone, add cooked spagetti shapes to the stock and then a few grated root vegetables – carrots and so on. Dice a courgette and a scattering of mushrooms. Add chopped French beans – even the remains of last night's pasta. Tag on a satisfying squidge of tomato paste, chopped parsley or celery tops and crown with a comforting blanket of parmesan. Serve in a big old-fashioned soup bowl and you have another 15-20 minute meal, tailor-made for a light Sunday lunch and so cosy the family are convinced you have spent the entire morning glued to the chopping board. You don't need to tell them that you have just emerged half an hour ago from a morning in bed with the papers and the Archers on Radio 4.

The children always tease me for being a "War Baby". It may sound funny to them, but those days of food shortages in the 1940s and early 1950s instilled a sense of frugality into the preparation of food. I hate waste. Leftovers at the end of a meal are put in the fridge to be used up in other dishes. Thus, the last portion of a chicken fricassee can make the basis for a soup. Melt a few chopped onions in butter, add last night's potatoes, some fresh chopped herbs and a litre or so of stock to make a perfectly respectable vegetable soup, which can be served either chunky or put in the liquidizer for a smoother consistency. Lots of leftovers can be utilized in this way. It is a satisfying challenge for the cook. My friend Sarah Orme coined the phrase "Fridge Art" and Fridge Art soup is served frequently in the Dyson kitchen. Often the family are not aware that what they are eating for lunch is the soupy version of the previous day's supper with additions, such as Tabasco sauce to change the flavour. In these days of ardent recycling, it seems that Fridge Art will become increasingly important.

Every Christmas our street of shops runs an open evening to raise money for the local old people's hospital. I used to make enormous pots of smooth vegetable soup – parsnip and curry, leek and potato, or carrot and orange. We set a small table on the pavement outside and the local families brought their children for their mugs of soup and chunks of bread – it worked a treat. Now with a clutch of restaurants, a deli and food shops who have come to our street in recent years, there are plenty of people serving food for the Christmas street party so we do a children's lucky dip instead.

Soup is also the staple for our annual boat race party, if the race is at lunchtime. It suits itself to all ages and is one of the easiest meals to serve on a cold day. There is usually a choice of two, served in mugs with ciabatta and slices of wholemeal bread. Then the Oxford and Cambridge fans can munch on an assortment of cheeses and fruit before they cheer the crews from our kitchen balcony.
In summer, creamy cold avocado soup is one of those easy

favourites that can be made when you get home from work – long live the liquidizer. As a dinner party overture, soup is ideal. You can cook it in advance. It looks spectacular in an antique tureen. There is also something homely about ladling it out at the table.

The trick with soup as a first course for a dinner party is not to be over-generous so you fill everyone's bellies too fast and leave no room for the main course. Victorian and Edwardian books on table service discuss this and advise that a soup bowl should be no more than half full, and that the soup should be eaten with a table spoon. In "Manners and Rules of Good Society," written by "A member of the Aristocracy" in 1895, the author advises: "Soup is nothing if it is not hot, and as it is the custom to give but a very small help of soup – about half a ladleful to each person – it is eaten quicker, and therefore hotter, with a large spoon than with a small one"

A 1920s book, "Etiquette for All", by Eileen Terry says: "Make no noise with the spoon, nor when swallowing the soup, which should not be scraped up from the bottom of the deep soup-plate, but skimmed up. As the liquid gets too low for this, you may tilt the soup plate, but be careful to raise the edge nearest to you, thus tilting the plate away from you. Take the soup from the side of the spoon, not from the tip, and begin to eat as soon as served, without troubling the other guests."

The old books also recommend against the serving of second helpings. These days it depends on who is dining – whether it is a hungry family sitting down for a scratch meal, or a more special dinner party with several courses.

Hearty lunch time soups need the partnership of chunky brown bread. Or heat something a bit continental like ciabatta or a baguette to munch with the soup. However, at the start of a supper party, it is not a good idea to fill everyone up too quickly, so with the soup, serve triangles of thin fresh toast, crisply fried croutons, or little wholemeal rolls.

Plain bowls of soup look more tempting with a garnish such as a scattering of well-chopped chives or parsley. Use a swirl of cream to decorate a smoother soup. Grated cheese works well on plates of chunky vegetable soups. The Victorians used rose petals to garnish delicate soups. Nasturtium flowers in sunny colours look happy on a dish of chilled gazpacho.

The soup recipes that follow are well-tested at home. They are gleaned from many years of family life in the kitchen. At the heart of all good soups is a good stock. The next part of this preamble gives suggestions for the home made variety, as opposed to the speedy convenience of the stock cube.

. . .

MAKING STOCKS

Victorian cookery books extol the virtues of the stockpot. Home-made stock was essential in every well-run 19th century (and earlier) kitchen. Much is written in old cookery books on clarifying stock, with recipes for all sorts of different types – veal, white stock, rich broth and so on. A heavy pot, simmering on the stove every day, gives promise of delicious meals to come. This is a supremely motherly pot, a pot to cherish and to dispense goodwill and love from.

The finished bones and leftovers go into my pot, especially the chicken, plus halved onions with their skins on to add flavour and a bit of colour. Root vegetables are chucked in, plus the remains of last night's vegetables or sauce - all this adds flavour. The pot is smartly boiled for 20 minutes or so every day while I'm doing pre-work kitchen tidying. Sometimes a pot keeps going for five or six days, with daily additions of bits and pieces of vegetable, herbs or added chicken scraps.

As a basis for soups, a good home-made stock is unbeatable. For sheer speed, though, there is nothing as convenient as organic instant stock cubes or powders – a kitchen essential that has its roots in coaching days when travellers needed food to eat in their carriages. Portable soup, or veal glue, as it was called, was the forerunner of today's stock cube – though the 19th century version did not contain monosodium glutamate. It was made from reducing the stock so much that it could be made into a paste, which could then be added to boiling water. I like the idea of stopping the coach en route to Bath, boiling the kettle over the fire, and making a quick warming cup of the Georgian forerunner of a stock cube.

In earlier days, the stock pot simmered permanently on the stove, being regularly refreshed with new ingredients. A Paris restaurant claimed its stock pot had been simmering for over 100 years. Today with women being unchained from the kitchen, a running stock pot can be more difficult to sustain.

Boil the stock up daily, then simmer for an hour with the lid on. If you boil the stock too fast, it will loose its translucency. Eject the vegetables daily, because they can go sour. Refresh with more onions, carrots, parsnips and or celery, depending on what is in the fridge. After a boil-up, strain the stock through a colander. Let it cool, then stick the bowl in the fridge. Several hours later, a well simmered stock will have jellied up. Skim the fat off the top and you have the base, not just for soups, but for sauces and stews. Even before straining, you can happily spoon out the hot stock directly into the day's soup, or pour it ladle by ladle into a gently cooked risotto. If the stock is fatty and you want to use it fast, pour it into one of those special jugs that drain the juices from the base, leaving the fat on top.

There are some simple rules for making stock. These apply to all the different types – chicken, beef, veal and so on. Beef is the best to use for a richer, brown stock and for stews and pot roasts. Use bones and chunks of meat, browning them first in the oven in order to give the stock a good colour. Use chicken (not forgetting the giblets which make a much richer and better tasting stock) and veal for a lighter stock. For fish stock, use bones, skins, head and either cooked or uncooked flesh. Home-made stock helps use food scraps much more economically. Nothing that comes out of a packet compares with your own stock.

GUIDELINES FOR SUCCESSFUL STOCK MAKING

1. Use either cooked or uncooked meat and bones, or a combination.

2. Chop the meat small, so plenty of the surface is in touch with the water – this helps flavour.

3. First bring the meat to the boil slowly with cold water. Boil fast for 10 mins and skim.

4. Now add vegetables and herbs – such as onions, parsnip, celery, carrots, garlic, parsley, bay leaves, thyme, marjoram etc., using the herbs sparingly. Leave the vegetables in chunks.

5. For a darker meat stock, brown the raw bones and meat in oil first, cooking fast, before adding the water.

6. If using cooked chicken bones and a carcase, lightly brown these in the oven before putting in the stock pot.

7. Once the vegetables have been added, after the stock has come to the boil, sprinkle in a good pinch or two of salt. Put the lid on the pan and simmer for three hours or more. Old books recommend six hours. Strain the stock and allow to cool, then refrigerate.

8. For a running stock pot, boil up the bones thoroughly for a minimum of 15 minutes a day – 30 is better. This keeps the pot fresh.

9. After two or three days, remove the vegetables, which can go sour and spoil the flavour if they are left in too long. If you want to keep the pot going, put in more vegetables or useful leftovers. Pour the stock into a clean bowl, using a sieve. Leave to cool and then refrigerate. The fat will rise to the top and can be skimmed off before the stock is used to make soups, sauces and gravies. However, the fat should be left on while the stock is stored in the fridge because it makes a seal and keeps it fresh. Stock can also be stored for later use if you seal it into a plastic bag and keep it in the freezer.

. . .

YESTERDAY'S COOKERY WRITERS ON THE SUBJECT OF STOCKS AND SOUPS

Francatelli, celebrated 19th century chef to Queen Victoria, writing in his 1861 recipe book: "The Cook's Guide, and Housekeeper's & Butler's Assistant" describes the stockpot as "The Very Soul of All Cookery". His thoughts on making stock are that "It ought never to be lost sight of, that good stocks, broths, gravies, and essences of meats, &c., are essential to the basis of all culinary compositions."

Mrs A.B. Marshall, whose popular Cookery Book was first published in 1887, wrote: "Stock, in some shape or other, is the foundation of all cookery, and on its quality depends almost entirely the excellence of any cuisine."

All sorts of soup recipes…

Serve soup in homely mugs if it is a smooth soup.
A chunky soup needs to be served in a bowl.

Soothing Fish Soup

This is an easy one to make, with simple ingredients and not too rich. It is also an excellent way of using up leftover fish and potatoes. To vary the flavour use other herbs such as parsley, bay leaves, finely chopped celery stalk and lemon hyssop. These are all good alternatives to the tarragon in this recipe. Make this when you get home, or cook the fish the night before you need to make up the recipe. It will keep in the fridge for 24 hours after cooking.

*"Beautiful Soup, so rich and green,
Waiting in a hot tureen!"*

Lewis Carroll – Alice's Adventures in Wonderland

500g white fish - haddock, cod, coley, roughey, or a mixture	A handful of tarragon
1/2 a litre milk	Grated peel of an orange
4 boiled potatoes or about 4 heaped tablespoons of mashed potato	25 - 50g butter (depending on how butter conscious you are) or a tablespoon of olive oil
	Fresh ground pepper and salt

Put the fish in a saucepan with the tarragon, half the milk, and seasonings. Simmer for about 10 minutes until the fish is cooked. Remove any skin and bones and discard. Put the cooked fish and all the rest of the ingredients, including the potatoes in the liquidizer and mix until smooth and like a thick cream. Return to the pan and heat to a gently bubbling simmer for about 15 minutess, adjusting the seasoning. You may need to add a little more milk if the texture is too thick. Garnish with a little sprinkling of chopped tarragon leaves and zest of orange and serve. Crisply fried brown bread croutons also work well as a topping.

*Serves 4

Barley & Vegetable Broth

This soup is what we call a soothy doothy – a simple and soothing doing – just right for a cold weather lunch, served with chunky bread for a chilly picnic. It was made first for our American friends, Mindy and Guy Durham, spending a cold winter day with us. This is the sort of recipe where you don't need to follow the ingredients slavishly. Be inspired by the contents of the vegetable drawer in your fridge. The barley enriches the soup and makes it more filling.

"One cannot make soup out of beauty."

Estonian Proverb

3 cloves of garlic, finely chopped	1 - 1.5 litres of home made meat or vegetable stock or use good instant stock
2 tablespoons of olive oil	
2 - 3 carrots, grated (about 1/2 a carrot per person)	Handful of chopped parsley
	3 - 4 handfuls of pearl barley
3 sticks of celery, including the top leaves, finely chopped	Seasoning - fresh ground pepper, salt and the juice of 1/2 a lemon
5 mushrooms, finely chopped	

Using a big heavy bottomed saucepan with a lid, heat the garlic, and other vegetables in the olive oil. Let them sizzle for a minute, then put the lid on and stew gently for about five minutes until they soften a bit. Make sure the vegetables don't brown. Add everything else. Bring the soup to boiling point and simmer for about 45 minutes until the barley has cooked. Adjust seasoning and serve with a sprinkling of fresh parsley.

Portion control: Work out a mug of liquid per person - about half a pint or a quarter of a litre. Refresh by simmering for 15 minutes, with more grated vegetables and stock added if wanted.

*Serves 6

BEAUTIFUL SOUPS by Kate Dyson

Curried Avocado Soup

This is a favourite summer standby. It couldn't be quicker to make before a meal organised at the last minute. On a hot day, the piquant chilled smoothness of the avocado and curry mixture is cooling. This soup also works well for special picnics. It travels and keeps chilled in a good vacuum flask. The lemon helps the avocado to keep its delicate green colour.

> *"People laughed at me when I said I did not want to dine at a tavern as one could not get soup there."*
>
> The memoirs of Casanova, after he visited London in 1763

1 litre cold chicken or vegetable stock (or 2 - 3 tins of best consommé)
2 avocados without skin and stones
2 tablespoons of olive oil
2 chopped cloves of garlic
1 dessertspoon of mild curry powder, to taste
Juice of 1 - 2 lemons
200ml single cream
Handful of chopped chives
A thin slice of avocado per person for garnish

Soften the garlic in the olive oil in a heavy pan for about five minutes – do not brown. Add the curry powder and fry gently for another two to three minutes to release the flavour. Mix in the stock, bring to the boil and simmer with the lid on for 15 minutes. Allow to cool, then place in the liquidizer with the avocados and lemon juice. Mix in the cream. Chill and serve with a swirl of extra cream, a sprinkling of well-chopped chives and a thin slice of avocado in the centre of each soup bowl. This soup looks especially pretty when served in old-fashioned glass finger bowls.

*Serves 4

Pumpkin Soup

This warming, homely soup needs bold flavouring. Let the family carve the pumpkin face for Hallowe'en and then use the flesh for making the soup. Slice the top off the pumpkin, scoop out its flesh, discarding the pips. Then use the pumpkin as the tureen when you serve the soup. Use home-made vegetable, chicken or beef stock if you have it. Otherwise a good quality organic instant stock will save time. This is a beautifully cheerful looking soup – ideal for a chilly late Autumn day.

"A first rate soup is better than a second rate painting."

Abraham Maslow

1 chopped onion	1 tablespoon butter
2 cloves finely chopped garlic	1 litre of stock
The chopped flesh of 1/2 a large pumpkin or 1 small one less than football sized	Seasonings - salt, fresh ground pepper, a tasting of chilli, and nutmeg.
1 - 2 heaped teaspoon of turmeric	Freshly grated Parmesan cheese to garnish
1 sliced large potato	For a richer version, add a couple of tablespoons of cream just before serving
1 sliced carrot	
2 tablespoons of olive oil	

Soften all the vegetables in the oil and butter with the turmeric. Put the pan lid on and sweat for about 10 minutes. Do not brown. Add the stock and other seasonings. Bring to the boil and simmer for about 20 to 30 minutes. Place in liquidizer to make a smooth consistency. Serve piping hot in soup bowls, garnished with a sprinkling of parmesan or a splosh of cream. Or bring to the table in the hollowed out pumpkin, using the top and stalk as a lid.

*Serves 6

Noodle Soup

If you have home-made stock of any kind, this is a warming way of making a quick lunch or back-from-work soup without much in the way of preparation. Serve it in little Chinese bowls with chopsticks. Add grated carrots, finely chopped celery and strips of crisp lettuce to pad it out.

"Only the pure in heart can make a good soup."

Beethoven

2 cloves of garlic
Tablespoon of olive oil
or of butter
1 litre home-made stock
or a stock cube

Soy sauce to taste
Pepper
2 sheets of easy
cook noodles
Chopped parsley or coriander

Soften the garlic in the butter or olive oil. Add the stock, the soy, the pepper and parsley and bring to the boil. Stick in the noodles and boil gently for five or so minutes until the noodles have expanded. Adjust seasoning. Serve in mugs with forks or in Chinese style small rimless bowls and matching spoons.

Variations – add roughly grated carrot, chopped celery leaves, finely chopped mushroom, a handful of peas or broad beans when you add the stock. Any or all of these will plump up the body of the soup. A handful of finely chopped chicken or of shrimps will also add more body.

*Serves 4 - 6

Bren's Fish Soup

You could call this cheating bouillabaise. It is a hearty lunchtime soup, quick to prepare and cosy to eat. It was made first on one of those cold and rainy days when you need to use up odds and ends from the fridge. Traditional bouillabaisse is a meal on its own. Although it originated in the South of France where the warm weather would perhaps call for something lighter and more cooling, this is full-on nourishment. You can make this as a smooth soup, or, by flaking the fish once it is cooked, it can be a more chunky version.

"I live on good soup, not on fine words."

Molière

1 onion	Tablespoon of tomato puree
2 cloves garlic	2 packets smoked haddock
1 medium sized fennel bulb	(4 standard fillets)
2 tablespoons of olive oil	3/4 of a litre of water
Handful chopped parsley	Paprika and fresh
2 - 3 bay leaves	ground pepper
Grated peel of an orange	Salt to taste, depending on
Tin of chopped tomatoes	saltiness of the haddock

Chop the raw vegetables and sweat in the olive oil for about 10 minutes in a deep pan with the lid on. Add everything else including the water. Bring to the boil and simmer for about 30 to 40 minutes until the vegetables are cooked and soft. Remove the bay leaves and liquidize. Return to the pan and heat. Serve with croutons covered with grated garlic and parmesan, plus an instant rouille, made from mixing a dollop each of mayonnaise and tomato ketchup, then seasoned with cayenne pepper.

*Serves 6

Coconut Chicken Noodle Soup

This is what you might call a cross culture soup. The pesto flavour blends well with the coconut milk to give a comforting herbal taste. This is a good soup to remember as a restorative for teenagers with hangovers.

"Soup puts the heart at ease, calms down the violence of hunger, eliminates the tension of the day, and awakens and refines the appetite."

Auguste Escoffier

1 standard large tin of coconut milk, full cream variety, not light, which tends to curdle when boiled	A tablespoon of fresh grated ginger
	2 cloves of grated garlic
	Splash of olive oil
1/2 litre of chicken stock	About 2 handfuls of finely chopped cooked chicken or prawns
Chopped coriander - handful	
3 - 4 tablespoons fresh pesto	
A good splosh of soy sauce	2 sheets of egg noodles

Toss the garlic and ginger in olive oil for a couple of minutes until softened and add everything else except the coconut milk and the noodles. Bring to the boil and simmer for about 15 minutes. Then add the noodles and simmer for a further five to 10 minutes. Now add the coconut milk and heat to simmering point. Season, adding salt and pepper to taste. Sprinkle a bit more coriander on the top before serving.

*Serves 4 - 6

Weekend Soup With Lemon Grass

Lemon grass is a welcome flavour that makes a refreshing change from the more predictable mixed herbs when added to this homely vegetable soup. It cleans the palate and gives a fillip of almost perfumed taste to this simple soup.

"You will still find people who believe that soup will cure any hurt or illness and is no bad thing to have for the funeral either."

John Steinbeck. East of Eden

1 litre of fresh home-made chicken stock that has been stewed with lemon grass.	2 pieces of lemongrass, cut in half lengthways
1 tablespoon of olive oil or butter	2 chopped courgettes
2 chopped leeks	1 medium peeled aubergine, chopped
1 chopped onion	2 cold boiled potatoes
2 - 3 cloves chopped garlic	2 handfuls of parsley
	Zest and juice of a lemon

Sweat the vegetables in the butter or olive oil for about 5 to 10 minutes with the lid on. Add the lemongrass and stock, boiling slowly for a further ten minutes. Remove the lemongrass. Then put everything in the liquidizer, adding the parsley and the lemon juice and zest. This will make it smooth and creamy. Return to the pan and bring to the boil, simmering for 15 minutes or so. Serve with a big dish of hot naan bread or freshly baked ciabatta, cut in tubby chunks.

*Serves 4 - 6

Courgette & Couscous Soup

This a speedy soup to make, especially if you are trying to use up remains from the fridge – just the thing to do with the last part of a roast chicken when there is not enough meat left to make a more substantial main course. The couscous helps to make it into a more substantial dish.

"The soup is never hot enough if the waiter can keep his thumb in it."

William Collier on Food and Eating

2 cloves of garlic, finely chopped	2 pints of stock or instant stock dissolved in water
1 - 2 chopped spring onions	Handful of chopped parsley
Splash of olive or sunflower oil	Teaspoon of turmeric
	Small teaspoon harissa paste (optional)
1 medium courgette	
2 - 3 tablespoons of couscous	Seasoning to taste

Melt the garlic and spring onions in oil for a few minutes. Add the turmeric and harissa paste. Fry gently with the onions for a couple of minutes to release the flavour. Add the stock and bring to a gentle boil. Roughly grate the courgette. Add this and the couscous to the hot stock. Bring back to the boil and simmer for about 10 minutes. Add the parsley after about five minutes. Adjust seasoning and serve.

*Serves 4 - 6

Wedding Plan Soup

We were planning a daughter's wedding with a complicated meeting around the kitchen table plus prospective son-in-law – known as Sil. The meeting went on longer than planned and all of a sudden supper had to be produced. It involved an instant menu concocted from the previous day's leftovers and other bits and bobs in the fridge and store cupboard. The previous evening we had had fish fillets baked with butter, lemon and parsley and there were about three left as someone had not turned up for supper. Also lurking in the fridge were the remains of the rice that was made for the same meal…
making an ideal base for a nourishing instant soup.

"A page of my journal is like a cake of portable soup. A little may be diffused into a considerable portion"

James Boswell

2 - 3 cooked portions of white fish	Teaspoon of curry powder
A tin of full fat coconut milk	Fish stock cube (optional)
1 garlic clove	1 cup or more to taste of fresh milk
3 chopped spring onions	2 cups of cooked rice
1 tablespoon of olive oil	Handful of chopped coriander

Soften the chopped garlic and onions in the olive oil, using a deep frying pan with a lid. Add the curry powder and cook gently for about 5 minutes so that the curry releases its flavour. Do not brown. Meanwhile liquidize the fish and coconut milk. Add contents of liquidizer to the pan, plus the seasoning, milk to taste, plus a stock cube if desired. Now add the cooked rice and bubble up gently for about five minutes until the rice is well heated. Sprinkle the chopped coriander leaves on the top and serve piping hot with naan bread or a freshly baked baguette with a crispy toasted crust.

*Serves 4 - 6

Chicken Broth With Parsley & Parmesan

This simple recipe is soothing as can be, with its roots in the 18th century, if not earlier, when eggs were sometimes used to thicken broth. The parmesan is a modern addition. It works well as a starter on cold evenings when you want something a little light on the stomach.

Got an invalid in the house? Then leave out the cheese, stick the broth in a mug and make toast soldiers. Take it upstairs to the sickbed on a small tray, as comfort and restorative to whoever is prostrate with flu. Only rule – you must have good well-flavoured home-made stock – it tastes so much better and has ancient health-giving properties.

"Worries go down better with soup than without."

Jewish Proverb

1 litre chicken stock,
clarified and well boiled
1 egg, whisked
A handful of finely
chopped parsley or mixture
of light fresh herbs such
as lemon balm, hyssop
2 tablespoons of grated
parmesan cheese
Juice of a lemon

Mix a tablespoonful or two of the hot, but not boiling, stock into the whisked egg. Now add this to the stock in the pan. Bring to just below boiling point and mix in the herbs. Don't allow to boil because the egg will scramble and the mixture loose its smoothness. Spoon into bowls or soup cups and sprinkle with Parmesan. If on Florence Nightingale duty, deliver the soup mug on a small tray with a tiny posy of flowers, a big colourful table napkin and hot toast in triangles or soldiers for dipping.

Variations – Julienne: leave out the egg and cheese. Add to the stock roughly grated carrot and finely sliced onion, softened in butter for five to ten minutes. Carrot and courgette: As above with the carrot, then about 3 to 5 minutes before serving, add finely chopped or roughly grated courgettes. Rice: Add a finely chopped onion, which has been softened in butter for 5 to 10 minutes. Then add a mug of cooked rice. Bring to the boil and simmer for 5 to 10 minutes.

*Serves 4 - 6

Parsnip Soup

Parsnips have an insistent flavour, which blends well with curry. Choose this soup for a nourishing snack lunch on chilly days. Parsnips have been cultivated on vegetable patches for 2000 years. The Romans, as recorded by the cookery writer Apicius, considered the parsnip to be a delicacy. However, with the advent of the potato, it took a back seat. No traditional stew or roast is complete without a parsnip or two. It is one of my favourite ingredients because it makes a fine winter creamy soup or can be used happily in mixed vegetable soups where it blends comfortably with onions and carrots, adding its individual slightly mustardy strength to the flavour.

"Faire words butter noe parsnips."

English proverb, quoted in the 1639
edition of the Oxford English Dictionary

1 tablespoon of olive oil
100g butter
1 onion, finely chopped
2 cloves garlic, chopped
2 large or 4 small parsnips
1 potato (optional
for a thicker soup)
1 litre chicken or beef stock
(the beef will give a
more robust flavour)
1 teaspoon medium
Madras curry (optional)
salt and fresh ground
pepper to taste
1 - 2 handfuls chopped
fresh garden herbs
Single cream to dollop
when serving

Soften the vegetables in the olive oil and butter, using a deep shallow pan with a lid. Simmer for 5 to 10 minutes. Add the curry powder and sizzle for about a minute to release the flavour of the curry, stirring the mixture in the pan. Add the stock, bring to the boil and simmer until the vegetables are cooked – about 15 minutes. Put in the liquidizer and process until the mixture is smooth. Return to the pan. Season to taste. Serve in bowls, with fresh herbs and a dollop of cream on top.

*Serves 4 - 6

Celery Soup

Celery is reputed to be good for blood pressure. It was introduced to Britain from Italy in the 1650s and was first used in salads. The parsley-like top leaves can be chopped and used as a welcome herbal flavouring in all sorts of mixed soups. As a stand-alone soup though, celery has a wonderfully delicate and instantly recognizable flavour which comes out best with chicken stock rather than a more robust beef stock. Victorians enjoyed celery cooked in creamy sauces. Sometimes I make this soup just with chicken stock and sometimes with milk, which is more rich and creamy, especially if you add a small pot of cream shortly before serving. At table, serve the soup in deep bowls with a drizzle of cream and a sprinkling of a few more finely chopped celery leaves or chives, or with a scattering of grated Parmesan cheese.

"A spoon does not know the taste of soup, nor a learned fool the taste of wisdom."

Welsh Proverb

- 150g butter
- 1 tablespoon of olive or sunflower oil
- 1 finely chopped onion
- 1 potato peeled and chopped
- 5 sticks celery, scrubbed and chopped, with the green leaf tops removed and finely chopped, then reserved
- 1 litre chicken stock or milk, depending on which version
- Salt and pepper, a pinch or 2 of celery salt, ground coriander seeds or fresh ground nutmeg, to taste
- Juice of a lemon
- 4 tablespoons of cream or about four tablespoons
- Grated Parmesan for garnish (optional)

Soften the onion, potato and celery in the butter and oil. Cook gently for about 10 minutes. Add the stock or milk. Bring to the boil and simmer for 20 to 30 minutes or until the celery feels tender. Liquidize and return to pan. Add the lemon juice, the seasonings and the chopped celery leaves. Simmer for another five minutes. Add the cream and simmer gently for another couple of minutes. Garnish with the grated cheese.

*Serves 4 - 6

Courgette & Lemon Soup

Lemon is a refreshing flavour in this easy to make light soup. It's a useful recipe if there are too many courgettes on the allotment or vegetable plot. For those on a low salt diet, lemon is a highly necessary alternative because its acidic qualities have the same sort of taste-enhancing effect as salt.

Courgettes have such a mild taste that they need the injection of the lemon to strengthen their presence in a dish. Although seen on every vegetable shelf today, they did not become a popular vegetable in this country until relatively recently. Elizabeth David first brought courgettes to the attention of keen British cooks in the late 1950s when they appeared in her much read cookery books.

"Having a good wife and rich cabbage soup, seek not other things."

Russian Proverb

1 tablespoon of olive oil
2 finely chopped cloves of garlic or 3 chopped spring onions, including stalks
3 courgettes, washed, trimmed and roughly grated

1 litre chicken stock
Finely grated rind and juice of a lemon, or two
Seasoning to include an optional addition of freshly ground nutmeg

---

Soften the garlic or spring onions in the oil for a couple of minutes, being careful not to let it brown. Remove the garlic, but leave in the onions if you are using these instead. Add the stock, the lemon juice and rind plus the seasoning. Bring to the boil. Simmer for 5 minutes, then add the grated courgettes, bring to the boil again and simmer for another 5 minutes. Adjust the seasoning. Sometimes a little more freshly squeezed lemon juice is needed. For a smooth soup, simply liquidize after cooking and serve with a splosh of cream in the middle of the bowl. Accompany with hot toast.

*Serves 4 - 6

Green Pepper & Lettuce Soup

It was the middle of Summer and we were having our friends, Bob and Elisabeth to supper, to celebrate the buying of their new home. There was a glut of lettuces on the allotment. After a busy day at work, this was one of those last-minute meals, so the challenge was to see what was in the fridge and turn it into something that tasted tempting. Assembled eaters gave a thumbs up.

"Memories are like mulligatawny soup in a cheap restaurant. It is best not to stir them."

PG Woodhouse

1 tablespoon of olive oil	1 medium-sized lettuce - then torn into bite-size pieces
2 cloves garlic, chopped	1 litre chicken stock
1 onion, finely chopped	2 handfuls chopped parsley
2 - 3 green peppers, chopped, de-seeded, skinned	Seasoning - salt and freshly ground coriander seeds and pepper
1 panful of fresh cos lettuce leaves, washed - equivalent to	

Soften the onion, garlic and green peppers in the olive oil, being careful not to let it brown. Add the lettuce and cook briskly for 2 to 3 minutes, stirring. Add the stock. Bring to the boil and simmer for 5 to 10 minutes, until the vegetables have softened and are cooked. Add the parsley leaves and liquidize furiously until the soup is as smooth as possible. Return to the pan. Reheat and season to taste. If the colour of the soup is a bit pallid, add a drop or two of green colouring. Serve with a dollop of cream and chunks of hot ciabatta bread.

*Serves 4 - 6

Mixed Vegetable Soup

This soup reminds me of my mother. It is homely and comforting. Serve it either smooth by putting it in the liquidizer, or as a chunky soup. After a chilly morning working in my parents' Yorkshire nursery garden, we would come in for lunch, hands filthy from weeding (gardening gloves were considered a bit namby pamby) and snatch a mug of Mum's soup, propped up by the Aga in the orange painted kitchen with its Magic Roundabout wallpaper. The vegetables you use in the soup should vary according to the season, so it is not laid down in stone that you must combine carrots and onions, or onions and parsnips with sweet potatoes. Trust your taste buds and enjoy combining different vegetables according to whim.

> *"I believe I once considerably scandalized her by declaring that clear soup was a more important factor in life than a clear conscience."*
>
> Saki

1 - 2 chopped cloves of garlic	Handful chopped parsley
1 - 2 finely chopped onions	Tablespoon of oil or butter
1 stick celery, chopped	1 litre vegetable or meat stock
1 - 2 carrots, chopped	Salt and fresh ground
1 - 2 finely sliced potatoes	pepper to taste

Gently heat the oil in a pan. Add all the vegetables and stir. Put the lid on then allow the vegetables to sweat for about ten minutes until they are soft, stirring occasionally, Add the stock. Bring to the boil. Simmer for about 20 minutes, until the vegetables have cooked. Adjust seasoning. For the chunky version, serve the soup in a bowl with a sprinkling of parsley.

For the smooth version, stick everything, including the herbs in the liquidizer and whizz until it becomes creamy. Re-heat and adjust the seasoning, then serve in mugs with croutons.

*Serves 4

Fridge Art Soup

The children tease me about the frugal eating habits of childhood, because I can't bear to waste food. When the chicken fricassée or the baked fish has a couple of uneaten helpings, I tend to use these as a basis for soups the following day. A friend, Sarah Orme, coined the phrase "fridge art". It means using up the leftovers. Once on a two-family holiday years ago with another friend Mindy Papp Durham, we decided that each day the previous day's remains would be incorporated into something we were eating – it was a challenge and I don't think anyone realized that, for example, the last helping of the previous night's shepherd's pie was incorporated into the pasta sauce. We turned soups into sauces. Potatoes were put into sautés and omelettes. Pasta remains were added to minestrones, kedgerees into fish soups and so on.

Rather that give a specific recipe, here are some guidelines for frugal soups, which can often be unexpectedly delicious.

"Old chickens make the best soup."

French Proverb

1. Cover the leftovers with a lid – an upside down saucer or plate is fine. I am not a great fan of cling film and would rather use foil if I have to, or a plate as a food cover. This way the food does not dry out.

2. Unless you have something in a strong sauce – fish, chicken or meat – start by softening chopped onion or a leek and garlic in butter or olive oil. One onion is fine as the base for a soup for four people. If you are doing a fish-based soup, add a chopped small bulb of fennel, or celery.

3. Add the leftovers, chopping everything into small, bite-size pieces.

4. Add appropriate stock – fish, meat, or vegetable – or milk if you want a more creamy soup. You need a good mug full per person.

5. Now add more flavouring if you feel the soup needs a bit more oomph. (recipe continued overleaf)

(fridge art recipe continued…)

Here is a list of suggestions for ingredients to develop the soup.

Tomato puree
Chilli powder
A small handful of porcini, soaked in hot water
Chopped herbs - parsley, marjoram, hyssop, lemon balm, oregano, thyme, lemon grass
A good dash of Worcestershire sauce
Tabasco sauce
Soy sauce
A little curry - this needs to go in before you add the meat. It should be fried in the oil for a minute or two, stirring, to mature the flavour.

A teaspoon of turmeric - treat in the same way as the curry above.
A handful of cooked rice
A handful of cooked pasta
Noodles
Finely chopped cabbage or crisp lettuce like butternut or romaine - a minute or so before serving
Juice of a lemon
A dash of sherry
Saffron
Grated Parmesan or pecorino cheese
Dollops of cream on serving
Croutons - added on serving

If you want a smooth soup, liquidize the mixture, but don't liquidize something with pasta or noodles in. It doesn't work. However rice and potato work well. When you are preparing a smooth soup, add the herbs when you put the mixture into the liquidizer. Return the mixture to the pan. Bring to the boil and simmer for five minutes or more, making timing allowances for any extra vegetables that you might have added. For a chunky soup, make sure the ingredients are chopped to a uniform size.

Suggested Garnishes.....

Croutons - use in smooth soups and clear soups	Dots of truffle oil
Finely chopped herbs - parsley, dill, marjoram, chives, coriander, basil (torn not chopped to preserve flavour), hyssop, celery tops	Crisp-fried slivers of onion and/or bacon
	Crème fraiche
	Sour cream
	Nasturtium flowers
	Rose petals
Slivers of lemon zest	Tiny slivers of crisp lettuce
Grated carrot	Lumpfish caviar
Dollops of single cream - for smooth soups	Grated cheese
	Tiny diced tomato flesh

Tomato Soup

The distinctive flavour of tomato soup takes me straight back to childhood suppers in my grandmother's Dorset kitchen, where I would be put on a high stool at the old pine table beside the cosy Aga. In the shop, it is one of my staple lunches, plus a couple of oatcakes. Like chicken soup, tomato is full of health giving properties, an excellent one to be sipped when you are feeling under the weather. Tomatoes have antioxidant properties which help the immune system to sweep away germs.

The quickest way to make tomato soup is to sweat a chopped onion and a couple of cloves of garlic in olive oil and butter, then to add a tin of chopped tomatoes. Stick the lid on and simmer for about 20 minutes, adding pepper, a little salt and a teaspoon of sugar to calm the acidity in the tomatoes. For a thinner soup, add a mug of meat or vegetable stock. Liquidize. Bring to the boil and serve with croutons. When there is a glut of tomatoes from the allotment in the Summer, or they are cheap in the farmers' market, then this more time consuming recipe which involves action in the slicing and dicing department, pays dividends with the taste buds.

1 onion chopped	1/2 - 1 litre chicken or vegetable stock
2 cloves garlic chopped	
1/2 kilo of tomatoes, peeled, de-seeded and chopped	A cup full of cooked rice
	Basil leaves to garnish
A tablespoonful of olive oil and a tablespoonful of butter (or 1 - 2 tbspns olive oil if you are watching your cholesterol)	Salt and pepper
	A teaspoonful of sugar
	Dollops of cream to garnish

Soften the onions and garlic in the oil and butter. Add the tomatoes. Cook gently with the lid on for about five minutes. Now add the rice and simmer for another five minutes, so the rice absorbs the tomato juices. Add the stock. Put in the seasoning. Bring to the boil and simmer for about 15 minutes. Adjust seasoning. Serve in bowls with dollops of cream and a fresh basil leaf or two to decorate the centre of the plate. Grated cheese also works well as a garnish because tomatoes and cheese are a perfect marriage of tastes. This can also be turned into a smooth soup, simply by putting in the whizzer.

*Serves 4 - 6

Tomato & Fennel Soup

The piquant flavour and colour of the tomatoes spruce up the taste of this homely soup. The complementary gentleness of the fennel tones down the acidity of the tomatoes and makes a delicious partnership in a gentle and perfectly soothing mixture. This soup was one that started out on a day when the fridge was not as full as it should have been and and all that the vegetable drawer could produce were the tomatoes and the fennel.

> *"Hot soup at table is very vulgar; it either leads to an unseemly mode of taking it, or keeps people waiting too long whilst it cools. Soup should be brought to table only moderately warm."*
>
> Charles Day, "Hints on Etiquette", 1844

1 onion, chopped
1 - 2 cloves of garlic, chopped
Tablespoon of olive oil
Tablespoon butter
6 ripe tomatoes, seeded, peeled and chopped
2 bulbs fennel
1 litre fresh chicken stock or a litre of water and a couple of teaspoons of instant stock
Salt and pepper
Tablespoon or small tub of crème fraiche
Finely grated orange zest to garnish

Melt the the onion, garlic, tomatoes and fennel in the olive oil and butter. Use a wide, deep frying pan for this with a lid on to keep in the steam as the vegetables soften. After about ten minutes of gentle cooking, the vegetables should be softened. Add the stock and seasoning. Bring to the boil. Place lid on pan and simmer for about 20 minutes until the vegetables are cooked through. Leave to rest for about five minutes and liquidize until smooth. Return to the pan. Re-heat to gentle boil. Adjust seasoning and stir in the crème fraiche to taste. Garnish with a sprinkle of orange zest. Serve with hot slices of one of those exciting brown loaves with olives or walnuts.

*Serves 4 - 6

BEAUTIFUL SOUPS by Kate Dyson

Lentil & Celery Soup

This soup is perfect for chilly winter days. The combination of the mildly crunchy celery slices works well with the lentils. Chilli flavouring gives a punch to the tastebuds, whilst the soothing tomato and chicken broth is the final ingredient to a thoroughly healthy dish.

"Of all the items on the menu, soup is that which exacts the most delicate perfection and the strictest attention."

Auguste Escoffier

1 onion, chopped
2 cloves garlic, chopped
3 - 4 stalks celery, chopped
2 tablespoons of olive oil
1 tin of lentils in tomato juice
1 litre of chicken stock, or stock cube

Chilli flavouring, or Tabasco sauce
1 tablespoon of tomato puree
Salt and pepper
Handful of chopped parsley, with the chopped leaves from the celery stalks

---

Soften the onion, garlic and celery in olive oil for about five minutes. Strain the tinned lentils. Add them plus the chicken stock to the onion in the pan. Bring to the boil. Add the tomato puree to enrich the tomato flavour. Add the chilli and the other seasonings to taste. Add more tomato puree if necessary. Stir and simmer for about ten minutes until the celery is cooked through. Scatter in the chopped parsley and celery leaves. Serve hot with wholemeal rolls or fingers of toast.

*Serves 4 - 6

Curried Apple Soup

This is John's recipe, made as a surprise one evening when I was working late in the shop and we had friends arriving at short notice. It's an unusual mixture – a good Autumn soup. Parsnip and apple soup is a traditional English recipe. John's version, without the parsnips, is lighter in flavour. The curry works well as a flavour enhancer.

"An idealist is one who, on noticing that a rose smells better than a cabbage, concludes that it will also make better soup."

H.L. Menken

A mug of stewed apple,
cooked without too much
water or sugar
1/2 of chicken stock
1.5 tablespoons curry powder

Small pot of cream
Juice of a lemon
2 peeled and chopped
garlic cloves
1 tablespoon of olive oil

Soften the garlic cloves in the olive oil for a few minutes. Now add the curry powder and stir briskly turning the flame up until the curry sizzles a bit – no more than a couple of minutes. Be careful not to burn it. Add the chicken stock and the stewed apple. Bring to the boil and simmer for 10 minutes. Puree and add lemon juice. Return to pan and re-heat. Have a good taste and adjust the seasoning with salt and pepper. Either add the cream now or dollop on to the centre of each plate when serving the soup.

*Serves 4

Hedgehog Soup

When the children were small I ran an antiques newspaper and used to write special features on food and antiques, finding old recipes and then serving them in the dishes in which they would have originally been presented. This soup was found in an 18th century cookery book. It is almond flavoured and the hedgehogs are made from small circular rolls decorated with split almonds like spikes, which are floated one in each bowl when the soup is presented at table. Almond soup has a long history dating back to 16th century Spain, where it is a traditional starter to the Christmas feast. Recipes for this soup are found right across European cuisine, from Italy across to England and from there on to late 19th century America. This soup is a gentle one with a tender and interesting flavour.

"What an awful thing life is. It's like soup with lots of hairs floating on the surface. You have to eat it nevertheless."

Gustave Flaubert

1 tablespoon of butter
or olive oil
Finely chopped onion
2 finely chopped garlic cloves
200g ground almonds
1 litre fresh chicken stock
Grated rind of a lemon
Mace to taste

Seasoning - salt and
fresh ground pepper
Juice of a lemon
Small pot of pouring cream
4 - 6 small circular
brown bread rolls
A packet of blanched
almond "spikes"

Soften onions and garlic in the oil or butter. Do not brown. So cook gently. Blend the ground almonds into this mixture. Add the hot stock slowly stirring it in. Add the lemon rind, seasoning and mace, plus the lemon juice. Simmer for about 15 minutes until onions and garlic are cooked. Liquidize in the blender until smooth. Return to pan ad bring to simmering point. Be careful not to let it get to a brisk boil. Stir in the cream to taste. Adjust seasoning again.

Heat the rolls and quickly place the almonds on the top of the bread rolls so they resemble hedgehog spikes. Now dole out the soup into individual bowls. Float a "Hedgehog" in each bowl and serve with a flourish.

*Serves 4 - 6

Minestrone

Long, slow cooking plus a handful of grated Parmesan, scattered in at the last minute, give this classic Italian soup its unique flavour. Tomatoes add colour to the soup, which is so thickly crammed with vegetables that it makes a lunchtime meal in itself. In my fridge there is usually a small cache of Parmesan rinds which I keep especially for putting into stocks for soups like this because it adds to the flavour. The whole point of this soup is to put in generous quantities of ingredients so that it becomes more like a meal than a runny soup with a few bits in. There are many minestrone recipes and each good Italian mother has her own. This is my motherly version.

"Soup and fish explain half the emotions of human life."

Sydney Smith

1 tablespoon of olive oil
1 tablespoon of butter
2 tablespoons chopped pancetta or ham pieces or smoked bacon, snipped into small pieces
2 chopped onions
4 chopped cloves of garlic
3 chopped pieces of celery
2 large carrots, chopped
Tin of borlotti or butterbeans, strained
2 litres of home made stock or stock powder
Tin of tomatoes, strained and chopped or 4 large tomatoes, skinned, de-seeded and chopped
2 finely chopped courgettes
2 handfuls of French beans, cut in half
2 handfuls fresh or frozen peas
1 - 2 mugs cooked pasta shapes or 1 cup long grain rice, cooked
1 - 2 mugs of sliced Savoy cabbage
Salt and fresh ground pepper
1 tablespoon of chopped mixed fresh herbs
A piece of Parmesan rind (optional)
2 tablespoons of grated Parmesan cheese

Note: These amounts and vegetable contents can be adjusted, depending on the season and your vegetable drawer contents. You can also add diced potato with the other vegetables at the beginning.

(recipe continued overleaf)

(minestrone recipe continued from previous page)

Warm the oil and butter in a thick-based pan with a lid. Add pancetta, onion, garlic, celery and carrots. Put lid on and cook gently for about 5 to 10 minutes. Stir a few times to turn vegetables over and infuse them with the butter and oil mixture. Do not burn. Add stock and tomatoes, borlotti beans and courgettes, together with rice or pasta and the Parmesan rind. Bring to boil and simmer for 1 to 2 hours. About half an hour before you serve the soup, add the cabbage, beans and peas. I prefer to add these ingredients quite late on in the cooking so they retain their greenness, although a true Italian Mama will have added them earlier in the cooking process. Just before serving, add a handful of Parmesan. Serve the rest of the Parmesan – and more – in a little dish at the table.

*Serves 4 - 6

"It [soup] is to a dinner what a portico or a peristyle is to a building; that is to say, it is not only the first part of it, but it must be devised in such a manner as to set the tone of the whole banquet, in the same way as the overture of an opera announces the subject of the work."

Grimod de la Reyniere

French Onion Soup

Johnny onions he was called and every year he would come wearing his Breton uniform of blue beret and faded blue shirt and trousers. He wheeled his elderly bicycle, decorated with strings of golden onions and fresh white garlic, down the street. Doors opened and the local housewives appeared for their annual onion fest. Alas, the computer age seems to have put paid to this old-fashioned door-to-door salesman. There is apparently only one French onion seller left who comes across the Channel regularly with his bicycle. By way of a nostalgia trip and because it is an old family favourite, here's my French onion soup recipe. The quality of the beef stock makes a difference to the final flavour of the soup. It looks delicious when served in individual earthenware bowls, with the bubbling toasted cheese on top.

"It [soup] breathes reassurance, it offers consolation; after a weary day it promotes sociability...There is nothing like a bowl of hot soup, its wisp of aromatic steam teasing the nostrils into quivering anticipation."

Sydney Smith

1 tablespoon of olive oil	1 tablespoon flour
1 tablespoon of butter	3 - 4 tablespoons dry sherry
700g onions, finely sliced	Salt and pepper
4 cloves of garlic, sliced thickly	To Serve:
1 litre good fresh beef stock, or cubes, or use tins of best beef consomme	4 pieces thick cut French bread, toasted
	2 tablespoons grated Gruyere or Parmesan cheese
1 dessertspoon sugar	1 tablespoon Cognac

Bring the stock and sherry to the boil and simmer. Meanwhile in a large frying pan, warm the olive oil and butter. Add onions and garlic, cover and stew gently until golden – about 20 mins. Remove the pan lid and the garlic, which tastes bitter when browned. Sprinkle sugar over onions. Turn up heat and stir frequently as the onions caramelize. Turn off the heat and sprinkle flour in. Stir. Then slowly add the bubbling stock, taking care that the flour is incorporated smoothly. Adjust flavouring and season. Simmer for about 30 minutes. To serve: Add cognac. Divide soup into four bowls. Float a piece of hot toasted bread in each bowl and top with grated cheese. Place under a hot grill for 3 to 4 minutes until the cheese bubbles.

*Serves 4 - 6

BEAUTIFUL SOUPS by Kate Dyson

Borscht

The Ancient Greeks considered beetroot to be a precious treasure and presented one to Apollo in his temple at Delphi. Apicius, the famous Ancient Roman cookery writer, was also a beetroot fan and included a recipe for the precious vegetable in his cookery book. No beetroot soup for Apicius – he advocated serving it with honey and wine. Historically a beetroot was considered to have medicinal properties. It was grown to heal people rather than to grace the table. Nowadays it has recently been discovered that beetroot juice can help to bring good health because it is said to lower blood pressure. This goes to show that old remedies often worked and that it is worth investigating the medicines of the old world. As the growing of this vegetable, originally found on the shoreline of ancient Greece, spread across Europe gradually, it began to be taken into the kitchen. By the 16th century, the Eastern Europeans were growing beetroot. It was in this area – the Ukraine, Russia, Poland – that the first recipes for beetroot soup, or borscht, have their origins. Each country has its own version – with sour cream, with yoghurt, served hot, served cold, with tomatoes, without tomatoes, with bacon. This is my version…

Approx 1 kilo cooked beetroot, sliced	Juice of a lemon
2 tablespoons of olive oil	About 3/4 of a litre of home made meat or vegetable stock
2 onions, peeled and chopped	Or use a stock cube
2 cloves of garlic, chopped	1/4 litre of milk
1 potato, peeled and sliced	Natural yoghurt or sour cream to garnish
1 carrot, peeled and sliced	
1 large bay leaf	Finely shredded young beetroot leaves to garnish
Salt, pepper, coriander, to taste	

Warm the olive oil in a deep pan. Add the onions, garlic, potato and carrot. Put the lid on and cook gently, turning occasionally, for about five minutes until the onions are transparent. Add the beetroot and the stock. Bring to the boil. Simmer for about 20 minutes or until all vegetables are softened and cooked through. Liquidize. Return to the pan. Add seasonings to taste. Finally add the milk, which is optional. The less liquid you add, the thicker the soup and I prefer a thicker version. Use dollops of cream or yoghurt to decorate the centres of each soup plate when it is served. Serve chilled or hot.

*Serves 4 - 6

Gazpacho

The Moors brought the origins of gazpacho to Spain in the middle ages. Medieaval gazpacho was made with stale bread, olive oil and vinegar and was a nourishing and refreshing meal for farmers. Tomatoes and peppers did not feature until they were discovered post Columbus. Like borscht, gazpacho has its regional variations in Spain. Other tomato growing countries have their local versions, but under different names. I first discovered gazpacho in the Alice B Toklas cookbook. My nearly 50 year old Penguin copy with yellowing pages is much thumbed, its corners dented with use. Miss Toklas gives seven versions, from different regions. All have garlic, tomatoes and olive oil, but not all have bread. Some are made with stock, cream and cornflour, but none have ice cubes, which seem to be a modern ingredient.

Here is my version. Make sure you use properly ripe tomatoes. I always keep my tomatoes on a sunny windowsill, which helps bring out their true flavour. Fridge-kept tomatoes straight from the supermarket often are tasteless.

1 kilo of ripe tomatoes	A cup of best olive oil
4 spring onions	1 teaspoon sugar
3 cloves of garlic	Water or cold consomme to
A small cucumber	taste in order to make the
1 green pepper	soup thinner in consistency
1 red pepper	Finely chopped green
2 tablespoons red wine	pepper to garnish
or sherry vinegar	Seasoning to taste

Peel, de-seed and roughly cut the tomatoes. Roughly chop the onions. Squish the garlic before peeling (this releases the juice). Peel and de-seed the cucumber. De-seed the peppers. Place all these ingredients in the liquidizer together with the vinegar, oil, seasoning and sugar. You may need to do this in more than one batch. Whizz until everything is as smooth as can be. Place in a large bowl. Add the water or consomme as needed if you want to make the soup thinner. Place in tureen or large bowl and refrigerate for a couple of hours. This resting time improves the flavour. Garnish the big bowl with finely chopped green pepper before bringing to the table.

*Serves 6

Bloody Mary Soup
– A Recipe From Marian Burros

Many years ago we were asked if we could help a friend of a friend, New York Times food writer Marian Burros, who was coming to London to review restaurants. She wanted someone to go with her on a tasting trip. Of course we said yes. It was the beginning of a lasting friendship, which saw me visiting Marian in Washington DC to buy antiques. These travels took us on long car journeys. We always felt we were escaping on our outings and ever since have called each other Thelma and Louise after the famous road movie. In return Marian would come to London and I was her driver for food writing trips, including an early investigation into organic meat which took us to Highgrove and on to Ludlow, with tasting sessions in the excellent restaurants there. Marian is a master of quick and delicious cookery. This recipe for a zingy chilled summer soup comes from one of her books "Pure and Simple – delicious recipes for additive-free cooking" – sadly not printed in the UK, though a fine book and warmly recommended by me.

1 medium onion, sliced	2 teaspoons
2 sticks of celery, diced	Worcestershire sauce
2 tablespoons butter	Salt and pepper to taste
2 tablespoons tomato puree	1 tablespoon lemon juice
720ml of tomato juice	120ml vodka

Sauté onion and celery in butter until golden. Add puree. Cook for one minute. Add the tomato juice and simmer for 10 minutes. Add the remaining ingredients. Cook for 1 minute longer. Strain. Return to the heat. Bring to the boil. Refrigerate at least 4 hours or overnight. Serve ice cold.

*Serves 4

"It is difficult to think anything but pleasant thoughts while eating a homegrown tomato"

Lewis Grizzard, American Comedian

Professica's Okra Soup
– Soupe de Gombos

We call her "Professica", but her real name is Jessica B Harris. A leading food historian, specialist in Afro-American cuisine, cookery writer and professor of French and English, Jessica divides her time between New York, New Orleans and Martha's Vineyard. I was staying in New York with a friend, Gray Boone, early in the 1990s. Jessica invited us to help her taste food at a restaurant she was reviewing. I don't remember when we ate, but I do remember that it was an evening of non-stop chatter. This was the start of a lasting friendship which has brought Jessica to London to stay with us, to go on antique hunts, to attend the Oxford Food Symposium and to become a family friend. This traditional French Caribbean recipe comes from her book "Beyond Gumbo – Creole Fusion Food from the Atlantic Rim".

480ml of chicken stock
480ml water
2 dozen okra pods, topped, tailed and cut into rounds

3 medium tomatoes, peeled, seeded and coarsely chopped
200g rice

Place the stock and the water in a heavy saucepan and bring to the boil. Add the okra and cook for ten minutes at low heat, stirring regularly. Place the tomato in a blender and pulse until you have a frothy liquid. Add the tomato mixture to the okra and stir until well mixed. Drizzle in the rice and cook for 20 minutes over medium heat, stirring occasionally. Serve hot.

*Serves 4 - 6

"Caribbean dining is all about food, friends and fellowship."

Jessica B Harris writing in her cookbook
"Sky Juice and Flying Fish, traditional Caribbean Cooking"

HISTORICAL NOTES

Soup is the most ancient of dishes on the menu, going back 5,000 or so years to when clay pots suitable for heating over a fire were first made. Originally you would have eaten a 'sop', which was a thick soup or stew into which pieces of bread were dipped to soak up the liquid. The liquid was known as broth or potage in Britain until the mid 17th century. It was poured on to the bread, which was used rather than a spoon.

The root of the word sop is prehistoric German – sup – which is also the origin of the word supper in English, soupe in France and zuppa in Italian. Up until the early 1700s, soup, or potage, was a substantial affair, in fact a whole meal. This changed in the early 18th century when soup began to be used as the overture to a meal with several courses.

Since pre-Elizabethan days kitchens would have had a stock pot kept topped up with meats and vegetables. It was called so literally because a 'stock' of soup was always on hand. It was essential to every kitchen.

Writing in one of the most famous cookery books of the earlier 19th century, Mrs. Marshall said that stock was the foundation of all cookery. Mrs. Beeton wrote that for economical cooking, a good stock pot should be found in every kitchen. George Leonard and Berthe E Herter in their extraordinary book "Bull Cook and Authentic Historical Recipes and Practices," published in 1960 by Herter's, produce a selection of adapted antique recipes, including a mid 18th century broth by the famous French chef, Boulanger, who opened the first ever restaurant. 'Restaure' was the French word for restore. Boulanger's restorative broth was cooked with pearl barley and garnished with red rose petals – worth a try.

The famous chefs of the 19th century, Alexis Soyer and Francatelli, both gave recipes for soup to be served to the poor. Soyer invented the camp stove and pioneered the feeding of the Irish during the potato famine with his nourishing yet inexpensive broth. He also travelled to the Crimea with Florence Nightingale and set up camp kitchens serving soups and stews to the literally starving British troops who had hitherto eaten disgusting, meager rations in appalling conditions. Francatelli, Queen Victoria's chef for many years, also gave a soup recipe for the poor in one of his books.

In the 20th century, Edwardian cook books contained recipes for rich, gamey soups and ladylike bouillons. French cookery was the pinnacle of culinary achievement, but with the influx of immigrants from other countries during the century, recipes started to contain more international ideas such as Russian bortsch and Spanish gazpacho.

Wartime cookbooks made the best of meagre rations by suggestions for cooking such questionable delights as oatmeal or cheese soup. Once food became plentiful again in the 1950s, there was the influence of Elizabeth David with her faithful recreations of French country and Italian soups and other recipes. Constance Spry's cooking created a rich country house atmosphere with suggestions like lobster bisque and chestnut soup – both recipes including liberal quantities of cream.

During my cooking life, nouvelle cuisine, cuisine minceur, Pacific Rim, and the power of the TV chefs has brought a global atmosphere to cooking, so the old recipes such as chicken soup have been rejuvenated with exotic ingredients like chillies and lemon grass – as easy to find now on the supermarket shelf as parsley. My mother would never have heard of either of these and my grandmother would never have looked for soup ingredients beyond her vegetable garden and the local butcher in Dorchester.

. . .

SOUP IS SERVED

In Medieval times soup would have been served from a bowl of pottery or wood. The grand Renaissance eaters would have used bowls of pewter, or even gold and it was not until Chinese porcelain was imported into Europe that a china bowl was used for soup. The early porcelain dishes were deep plates, deep enough to contain a dish with meat and gravy or a sustaining soup.

By the late 18th century, grand dinner services were being made all over Europe by the great china makers of the era and these would all have had soup bowls, as well as dinner plates. There was a Sèvres service for the French Royal Family in the 18th century. The delicate sprig Chantilly pattern, still reproduced today, was designed for Marie Antoinette, who undoubtedly would have supped her soup from the fine plates. There was the famous frog service, complete with imposing soup tureens made in creamware by Wedgwood for Catherine the Great, decorated with English views, and surmounted by a frog crest.

From the late 18th century onwards, grand families have ordered their own dinner wares. Wedgwood's pattern books still exist and the patterns he designed with their individual crests and delicate, yet often brightly coloured borders are on show in the Wedgwood museum in Barlaston – at the time of writing endangered by a pension funding problem following the collapse of the company.

Chinoiserie patterns, Etruscan styles, delicate botanicals – the different decorations on the soup plates reflect the current fashions, right up to the millennium when decoration became unfashionable and everyone seemed to want to eat using bare white plates, so the pattern would not detract from the artistic arrangement and colour of the carefully cooked food.

Soup today does not necessarily need to be served in those big old rimmed plates either. Use a mug, a cup and saucer, or even a finger bowl – great for a colourful cold soup. Little two handled soup cups with lids and matching saucers were fashionable in the 1930s and are now showing signs of popularity again on today's tables. Little starter soups, sometimes called amuses bouches, are served in dainty coffee cups, as an overture to a meal, to stabilize the palate.

I often put together "harlequin" services for customers – where each plate is different, but has a colour or pattern theme to hold the visual effect together. For one customer, there was a set of antique blue and white transfer plates, each one with a different pattern. For another, in America, the soup plates all had beautifully painted flowers as decoration. As an overture to a meal, these mixed sets look interesting on the table and make a line of conversation as guests compare the decoration on their plates. Also, if one gets broken, it is not the end of an expensive matching set.

...

THE SOUP TUREEN

Throughout the centuries the soup tureen has been a symbol of the bounty of the table and the power of the host. Elaborate soup tureens were made by the silver and porcelain manufacturers of the world. There were rococo tureens encrusted in swirls and flowers, neo classical tureens inspired by the designs of the ancient Greeks and Romans, as well as tureens designed for particular soups – such as pheasant. These would be borne to the dining room with ceremony. Many of the grandest can be seen in museums such as the Victoria and Albert in London and the Louvre in Paris, as well as in historic homes.

Simple earthenware or cast iron tureens were the centre of the farmhouse and pioneer table all over the Western world, containing rustic and reviving vegetable and meat soups.

There are periodic revivals of the fashion for simple country cooking, when homely soups are served in brown earthenware tureens. Elizabeth David was the leader with her book on French Provincial Cooking published in the mid 20th century and still in print. This inspired kitchen shop owners to hunt for simple pottery tureens and dishes, which were then filled with comforting onion soups. Mrs. David used to sell these everyday plates, which she brought over from France, in her famous London kitchen shop.

Today's soup tureens have sleek, minimalist lines. While you will see china and pottery tureens by the designers of the day, you are less likely to see them in silver, unless they are for ceremonial use in a livery company or for an inspired and well-heeled patron.

There are no hard and fast rules about what type of tureen to use or what sort of soup dishes. The main thing is to enjoy the cooking and serving of something that tastes good in the convivial atmosphere of the kitchen or dining room.

ACKNOWLEDGEMENTS

Thank you to my family, who have tasted these
soups at our kitchen table over the years....

John, Jemima, Titus, Jenny,
Nick, Jack, Kinna and Greg.

And to close friends, who have shared recipes,
sat round our kitchen table, read proofs
and given encouragement...

Sarah, Caroline, Mindy, Gray, Marian, Jessica,
Nic, David, Enid, Annie, Kathe and John.

Thank you also to Jenny's team at Pencil Agency
for graphic design work (pencilagency.com)
and to Nic Barlow for good advice on the cover.

As I was finishing the proofs for this book, John, my husband was suddenly struck by a vicious and incurable cancer. Some of the proceeds will be donated to the wonderful Princess Alice Hospice in Esher, where he was able to spend his final days in peace with the family gathered around.

WHERE TO FIND SOUP DISHES

Soup dishes, spoons, ladles and tureens can always be found in Kate's shop in Barnes, London. She established The Dining Room Shop in 1985. Since then customers from all over the world have visited the shop to enjoy the ever changing stock of antique and bespoke dining and kitchen furniture and related accessories, old and new.

The Dining Room Shop,
62 White Hart Lane,
Barnes,
London SW 13 0PZ

T: 020 8878 1020
E: enquiries@thediningroomshop.co.uk.
W: www.thediningroomshop.co.uk.